Summer Solutions.
Minutes a Day-Mastery for a Lifetime!

level 2

English Grammar & Writing Mechanics

Nancy McGraw & Nancy Tondy

Bright Ideas Press, LLC
Cleveland, Ohio

Summer Solutions Level 2
English Grammar & Writing Mechanics

All rights reserved. No part of this publication may be reproduced or transmitted in any form or by any means, electronic or mechanical, including photocopy, recording, or any information storage or retrieval system. Reproduction of these materials for an entire class, school, or district is prohibited.

Printed in the United States of America

ISBN 13: 978-1-934210-03-1
ISBN 10: 1-934210-03-x

Cover Design: Dan Mazzola
Editor: Kimberly A. Dambrogio

Copyright © 2008 by Bright Ideas Press, LLC

Cleveland, Ohio

Instructions for Parents/Guardians

- *Summer Solutions* is an extension of the *Simple Solutions Approach* being used by thousands of children in schools across the United States.

- The 30 lessons included in each workbook are meant to review and reinforce the skills learned in the grade level just completed.

- The program is designed to be used three days per week for ten weeks to ensure retention.

- Completing the book all at one time defeats the purpose of sustained practice over the summer break.

- Each book contains answers for each lesson.

- Each book also contains the *Help Pages* which list vocabulary, parts of speech, editing marks, and rules for capitalization, punctuation, and spelling.

- Lessons should be checked immediately for optimal feedback.

- Adjust the use of the book to fit vacations. More lessons may have to be completed during the weeks before or following a family vacation.

Summer Solutions Level 2
English Grammar & Writing Mechanics

Reviewed Skills include:

- Sentences/Subject/Predicate
- Punctuation
- Capitalization
- Editing Marks/Sentence Writing
- Compound Words
- Spelling Rules
- Nouns/Proper Nouns
- Pronouns
- Verbs/ Helping Verbs/ Irregular Verbs
- Synonyms/Antonyms/Homophones
- Plurals / Possessives
- Contractions
- Quotation Marks
- Adjectives

Help Pages begin on page 63.

Answers to Lessons begin on page 69.

Lesson #1

1. **The naming part of a sentence is also called the <u>subject</u>.**

    Underline the subject of the sentence.
    What is the sentence about?

    <u>A baby frog</u> is called a tadpole.

2. Underline the **antonyms** or **words that mean the opposite**.

    <u>heavy</u>   silly   kind   <u>light</u>

3. Choose the correct verb to show **past time**.

    Waves (crash / (crashed)) against the rocks.

    Courtney (smell / (smelled)) the flowers.

4. Drop the *e* before adding *-ing*.

    drive ➡ _driving_

    give ➡ _giving_

5. Every sentence begins with a _____ letter.

   (capital)   lower case

6. Write this sentence correctly.

   We are getting a $wimming pool in june⊙

   We are getting a swimming
   Pool in June.

7. Underline the correct verb.

   My sister (gave / given) me a puzzle book.

   I have (did / done) all of it already.

8. Circle the adjective that describes the underlined noun.

   Damian jumped over a (huge) puddle.

Lesson #2

1. **Another name for the action part of a sentence is the <u>predicate</u>. The <u>predicate</u> tells what the subject did or does.**

   Underline the predicate or the action part of the sentence.

   Noah <u>plays the drums</u>.

2. Add the prefix *un-* to the word below to make a word that means "not easy."

   un- + easy ➡ <u>uneasy</u>

3. Put quotation marks around what someone says.

   Mom said, "Make your bed before we go."

   Pedro asked, "Can I play with you?"

4. Write the two words that make up the compound word below.

   seashore ➡ <u>sea</u> + <u>shore</u>

5. **Add -er to adjectives to compare two people or things.
Add -est to compare more than two people or things.**

   Examples: Davita jumps <u>higher</u> than Ania.
   Kyra can jump the <u>highest</u> of all the girls.

   Choose the correct adjective.

   A fish is ((smaller) / smallest) than a shark.

   A flea is one of the (smaller / (smallest)) insects.

6. Fill in the correct end mark.

   Where is my hammer **?**

   I got a new camera **!**

   What a great picture **!**

7 – 8. List four adjectives to describe the penguins.

A) woke sib tosib   *walk side to side*

B) fluffy

C) beke   *has a beak*

D) webr fete   *webbed feet*

Lesson #3

1. **Another word for the action part of a sentence is the predicate. The predicate tells what the subject did or does.**

   Underline the predicate or the action part of the sentence.

   The parrot talks to us.

2. Underline the **subject** or the **naming part of the sentence.**

   The children took off their mittens.

3. Which word has a spelling mistake? Write the word correctly on the line.

   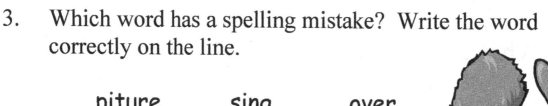

   piture   sing   over

   _____

4. Write the mark for "make capital." _____

5. Choose the correct homophone.

   An octopus has (ate / eight) legs.

   She (ate / eight) all of her pizza.

6. Write the words that make up each contraction.

   Nick doesn't feel well. _____ + _____

   We don't have any medicine. _____ + _____

7. Put in a comma and quotation marks.

   The nurse asked   How are you feeling?

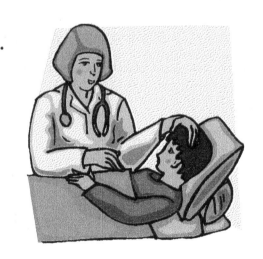

8. Add the suffix -less to the word below.

   spot + -less ➡ _____

Lesson #4

1. **Another word for the action part of a sentence is the <u>predicate</u>.**

   Underline the predicate or the action part of the sentence.

   The squirrel ran up the tree.

2. Underline the sentence.

   The path was narrow.

   Got lost.

3. Add some words to the one you didn't underline in item #2 to make a complete thought.

   _____

4. Circle the adjective that describes the underlined noun.

   Jenny put on her yellow <u>jacket</u>.

   We saw a spotted <u>whale</u>.

5. Underline the **subject** or **the naming part** of the sentence.

Some animals like to eat flowers.

6. Circle the **synonyms** or **words that mean the same**.

    tired   easy   lazy   simple

7 – 8. Write 2 or 3 sentences telling how to make an ice-cream sundae. Use words from the Word Box to help you.

ice-cream	fudge	cherry	spoon	bowl
	candy topping	whipped cream		

_____

_____

_____

_____

Lesson #5

1. Put in commas and quotation marks.

    Monica asked   How old is your dog?

    I answered   He's five years old.

2. Underline the predicate of the sentence.

    Tonya loves to play video games.

3. Choose the correct verb.

    This show (is / are) exciting!

    The children (is / are) cheering.

4. Choose the correct homophone.

    I picked a (bury / berry) from the tree.

5. Underline the subject of the sentence.

   My sister and I gave our aunt some flowers.

6. Use the marks for "add something" and "add a period" to fix this sentence.

   I like to eat fries with hamburger

7. Circle the adjective that describes the underlined word.

   The man had a loud voice.

   We drive a silver truck.

8. Add -s or -es to each word to make it mean more than one.

   beach ➡ _____

   couch ➡ _____

Lesson #6

1. **When a word ends in a consonant + -y, change the -y to -i and add -es to name more than one.**

    Change the -y to -i and add -es to each word.

    pony ➡ _____

    penny ➡ _____

2. Underline the verb.

    Jeff and his friends rode their bikes to the park.

3. Write a contraction for the underlined words. (Use the *Help Pages* if you need to.)

    Mitch <u>does not</u> like cats.   _____

    I <u>cannot</u> play golf.   _____

4. Which word means the same as the word *friends*?

        pals   pretty   team

5. Circle the correct verb.

   Jason (throw / throws) the ball.

   Dad (drive / drives) the van.

6. Use the mark for "take something out" and "add a period" to fix the sentence.

   My the dog always barks at strangers

7. Rewrite the sentence in item #6 correctly.

   _____

   _____

8. Choose the correct verb.

   I (am / is) going to the movies.

   Drew (was / were) on the bus.

Lesson #7

1. **The suffix -*less* means "without."**
   Example: The coin was worthless. The coin did not have any worth.

   Add the suffix -*less* to the word *hair* to make a word that means "without hair."

   hair + -less ➡ _____

2. Change the -*y* to -*i* and add -*es* to these words.

   puppy ➡ _____

   bunny ➡ _____

3. Underline the **subject** or **naming part** of the sentence.

   The baby smiled at me.

4. Write the two words that make up the compound word below.

   newspaper ➡ _____ + _____

5. Some verbs have a special spelling to show past time. They have another spelling when you use them with *have* and *has*.
   Example: <u>did</u> and <u>has done</u> / <u>had done</u>

   She <u>did</u> the wrong page.
   She <u>has done</u> the dishes already.

   Circle the correct verb.

   My sister (did / done) her homework.

   She has (did / done) a good job.

6. Which words have the same vowel sound?

   coat   saw   make   toad   time

7. Underline the nouns. (There are 2.)

   The bird is making a nest.

   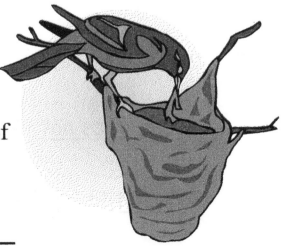

8. Use a pronoun to take the place of *The bird* in the sentence above.

   _____

Lesson #8

1. Add an *apostrophe* + *-s* ('s) to make a single noun show ownership.

   The brush belongs to Erin. It is Erin___ brush.

2. Underline the <u>telling sentence</u>.

   Wow, this is a mess! Please clean your room. Do you need a dust rag? I'll also bring the sweeper.

3. Underline the pronoun in each sentence.

   We ate donuts.

   She takes tennis lessons.

4. Replace the underlined words with a contraction.

   Sarah <u>does not</u> like cats. _____

   I <u>do not</u> know the answer. _____

5. Some verbs have a special spelling to show past time. They have another spelling when you use them with *have* and *has*.
Example: <u>gave</u> and <u>has given</u> / <u>had given</u>

Choose the correct verb.

Mario (give / gave) his book report.

Tony had (gave / given) his book report yesterday.

6. Add the suffix *-ful* to the word *play* to make a word that means "full of play."

play + -ful ➡ _____

7. Underline the predicate of the sentence. Then circle the verb.

Nicholas tossed the football to me.

8. **Whenever you write a paragraph, you should move over or indent the first word. This is the mark to show "move over" or "indent." (¶)**

Write the mark for "move over." _____

Lesson #9

1. Add the suffix *-er* to the word below to make a word that means "someone who dances." (Drop the final *-e* in the word *dance* before adding the suffix.)

   dance + -er ➡ _____

2. Fill in the end mark.

   Do you live near here__

   Skye fed the birds__

3. Change the *-y* to *-i* and add *-es* to name more than one.

   hobby ➡ _____

4. Underline the sentence that is correct.

   Susie and I jumped rope.

   I and Susie jumped rope.

5. Write the two words that make up the compound word *mailbox*.

   _____ + _____

6. Use the mark for "move over" or "indent" to fix this paragraph.

   Jared found a dollar on the ground. He ran home and told his mom. She told him to put the dollar in his bank. It was a lucky day!

7. Write the pronoun that could take the place of *Jared* in the sentence above.

   _____

8. Find three mistakes in the sentences below. Use the "special marks" to show how to fix them.

   Darla bought a book about birds she read ten pages as soon as she home.

Lesson #10

1 – 2. **Adjectives** are words that **describe** or **tell how something looks.** **Adjectives** can tell the **color, size, shape,** or **how many.** Use the chart to help you describe each fruit.

object	color	size	shape	how many
grape				
watermelon				

3. Use the marks for "make capital" to show which words should begin with a capital letter.

   my family went to the zoo on memorial day.

4. Which word has a spelling mistake? Write the word correctly.

   mothar   sister   often

   _____

5. Underline the subject of this sentence.

   My mom made us pancakes for breakfast.

6. Which word means the opposite of *dark*?

   light   sharp   color

7. **If a word ends in *-e* and you want to add a suffix that begins with a vowel, drop the *-e* before adding the suffix.**

   Example: (dive + -ing)   We took <u>diving</u> lessons.

   In each word, drop the *-e* before adding *-ing*.

   use + -ing _____

   smile + -ing _____

8. Underline the proper nouns in this sentence.

   Leo and Jackson live in Ohio.

Lesson #11

1 – 2. **Adjectives also tell how something tastes or smells. Example: Potato chips taste salty.**

Choose an adjective from the Word Box to describe each noun below.

| sweet | sour | juicy | hot |

cake ➡ _____   pickle ➡ _____

apple ➡ _____   chili sauce ➡ _____

3. For these nouns that name more than one, add an apostrophe <u>after</u> the -s (-s') to show ownership.

   the girls__ crayons   the birds__ cages

4. Add -s or -es to each word to make it name more than one.

   pencil - _____

   dish - _____

5. Underline the verb.

The sprinkler sprayed water on us.

6. Which word rhymes with *thing*?

   hug   swing   big

7 – 8. Draw a picture of your family in the box. Write 3 sentences that tell about your family.

A) _____

B) _____

C) _____

Lesson #12

1. **Adjectives** can tell how something **looks, feels,** or **sounds.**
   Examples: The oven feels <u>hot</u>.
   Those eggs smell <u>rotten</u>.
   That boy has a <u>soft</u> voice.

   Use an adjective from the Word Box in each sentence below.

   | hot   spicy   wet   sharp |

   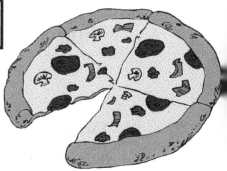

   The pizza tastes _____.

   My dog's nose feels _____.

2. Underline the nouns in this sentence.

   We collected seashells on the beach.

3. Write the two words that make up the compound word in item #2.

   _____ + _____

4. Nouns name people, places, or things.

   true   false

5. Choose the correct verb.

   I (is / am) invited to Doug's birthday party.

   We (was / were) going to sleep in a tent.

6. Write a contraction for the underlined words.

   Trina <u>cannot</u> find her jacket.   _____

   The teacher <u>is not</u> here today.   _____

7. Every sentence begins with a _____ letter.

   capital   lower case

8. Write the mark for "add a period."   _____

Lesson #13

1. Write a pronoun that can replace the underlined words.

   The mouse ran through the house. _____

2. Write this sentence correctly.

   Jake has a soccer game on sunday.

   _____

   _____

3. Circle the word that is a synonym for (means almost the same as) the word *fast*.

   slow   quick   jump

4. Underline the predicate of the sentence.

   Grace cooked turkey for dinner.

5. Write the verb in item #4 that shows past time.

   _____

6. Use any adjective to describe the puppy in this sentence. (Adjectives can tell how it looks or sounds.)

   A _____ puppy ran by my window.

7. Add the prefix *re-* to the word *say* to make a word that means "to say again."

   re- + say ➡ _____

8. Write the sentence that is a command on the lines below.

   We are having a bake sale at school. We will have chocolate chip cookies. Bring your money tomorrow.

   _____

   _____

Lesson #14

1. Choose the correct helping verb.

   Carrie (has / have) eaten her breakfast.

2. Use an adjective from the Word Box to describe each noun.

   | shiny   slippery   wet   fast |

   a _____ snake

   the _____ scooter

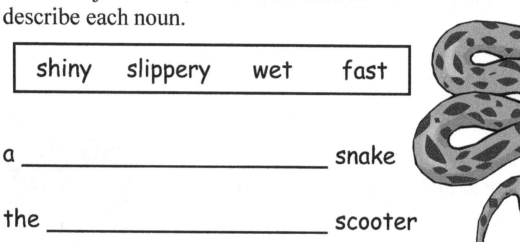

3. Which words have a long vowel sound?

   goat   tired   catch   better

4. Fill in the end mark.

   What a great game__

   Where did Gina go__

Summer Solutions© Grammar & Writing   Level 2

5. Write **Yes** if the word group makes a sentence and **No** if it does not make a sentence.

   A) I caught a fish. _____

   B) Has eight feet. _____

   C) The leaf. _____

   D) The sun melted the ice. _____

6. Use the mark for "make capital" and "add something" to fix this sentence.

   the monkey swung from tree.

7. Write the sentence in item #6 correctly.

   _____

   _____

8. Underline the proper nouns.

   Tyrone went to see Dr. Kendall.

Lesson #15

1. **Add -er to adjectives to compare two people or things. Add -est to compare more than two people or things.**

   Choose the correct adjective.

   His car is (faster / fastest) than mine.

   Allen's car is the (fastest / faster) of all.

   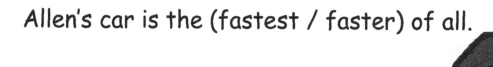

2. Underline the words that should begin with a capital letter.

   today   april   monday

   ice-cream   christmas

3. **If a word ends in -e and you want to add a suffix that begins with a vowel, drop the -e before adding the suffix.**

   In each word, drop the -e before adding -ing.

   save + -ing ➡ _____

   wave + -ing ➡ _____

4. Add an *apostrophe* + *-s* (*'s*) to the noun to show ownership.

The hamster belongs to Dexter.

It is Dexter___ hamster.

5. Write a pronoun that can take the place of the underlined words.

<u>Emily</u> went down the slide.   _____

<u>The kite</u> was caught in a tree.   _____

6. Change the *-y* to *-i* before adding *-es* to name more than one.

daisy ➡ _____

body ➡ _____

7 – 8. Circle the adjective that describes each underlined noun.

He likes spicy <u>tacos</u>.   The <u>flower</u> smells sweet.

The <u>table</u> was sticky.   I spit out the sour <u>candy</u>.

Lesson #16

1. Add *-er* to adjectives to **compare two people or things.**
   Add *-est* to **compare more than two people or things.**

   Choose the correct adjective.

   Fran's dog is (bigger / biggest) than mine.

   She has the (bigger / biggest) dog in the neighborhood.

2. Write the mark for "move over" or "indent." _____

3. Choose *has* or *have* to finish each sentence.

   Our game should (has / have) started already.

   Mason (has / have) done his exercises.

4. Underline the verb.

   We watched the fireworks from the window.

Summer Solutions© Grammar & Writing   Level 2

5. Underline the correct sentence.

    I and Jerry play basketball.

    Jerry and I play basketball.

6. Add *-s* or *-es* to make the nouns name more than one.

    match ➡ _____

    friend ➡ _____

7. Add the prefix *pre-* to the word *heat* to make a word that means "before heating."

    pre- + heat ➡ _____

8. Which word has a spelling mistake? Write the correct spelling on the line.

    buzy   white   school

    _____

Lesson #17

1. Circle an antonym for the underlined word.

   Shawna was <u>asleep</u> at the fair.

   tired   sleepy   awake   down

2. Which part of the sentence is underlined?

   Nate <u>needed help to shovel the snow</u>.

   naming part   action part

3. Use the mark for "add something" to fix this sentence.

   The turtle moved slowly across yard.

4. Rewrite the sentence in item #3 correctly.

   _____

   _____

5. Write this sentence correctly.

   mr. Williams is my football coach

   _____

   _____

6. Choose the correct adjective.

   The blanket is (softer / softest) than my teddy bear.

   It is the (softer / softest) blanket I have ever had.

7. Underline the nouns in the sentence. (There are 5)

   The boys brought a softball, some bats, and their gloves to the field.

8. Write the verb from the sentence in #7 above.

   _____

   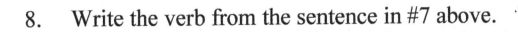

Lesson #18

1. Add the suffix *-ful* to the word *help* to make a word that means "full of help."

    help + -ful ➡ _____

2. **Homophones are words that sound alike but have different spellings and meanings.**

    Examples: <u>red</u> and <u>read</u>

    I bought a <u>red</u> balloon.

    My mom <u>read</u> me a scary story.

    Choose the correct homophone.

    The wind (blue / blew) the tree down.

    I (one / won) the lottery.

3. Write the mark for "add something."

    _____

4. Use the marks for "indent" and "add a period" to fix this sentence.

    We heard Sal blow the whistle

5. Write a proper noun for each word.

   city ➡ _____

   aunt ➡ _____

   state ➡ _____

6 – 7. Use an adjective from the Word Box to finish each sentence.

| green | hot | cold | wash |

We ate _____ sandwiches for lunch.

I also had a glass of _____ tea.

For dessert, I had some _____ grapes.

8. Circle the correct verb.

   Frankie (is / are) my next door neighbor.

   I (is / am) friends with Shawn, too.

Lesson #19

1. **Homophones** are words that **sound alike** but have **different spellings and meanings.** Choose the correct homophone.

   Please put away your (close / clothes).

   Mom needs (flower / flour) to make the cookies.

2. Underline the correct verb.

   Last week the boys (play / played) hockey.

   I saw the dog (wag / wagged) its tail.

3. Replace the underlined words with a contraction.

   Marlene is not going to win. _____

4. Drop the -e before adding -ing to each word.

   joke + -ing ➡ _____

   bake + -ing ➡ _____

5 – 8. Write 3 or 4 sentences telling what you did, or are going to do over your summer break. Be sure to indent; begin sentences with capital letters and end them with an end mark.

Lesson #20

1. Circle the word that means almost the same as the underlined word.

   My sister was very <u>mad</u> at my brother.

   angry   proud   scream

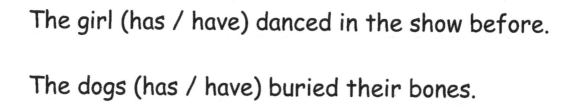

2. Choose the correct verb.

   The girl (has / have) danced in the show before.

   The dogs (has / have) buried their bones.

3. Circle the adjective that describes the underlined word.

   I put clean <u>sheets</u> on the bed.

   Tonya had silky <u>hair</u>.

4. Write the two words that make up the compound word.

   railroad ➡ _____ + _____

5. Choose the correct homophone.

   I (hear / here) a woodpecker.

6. Add the suffix *-less* to *clue* to make a word that means "without a clue."

   clue + -less ➡ _____

7. Write a pronoun that can replace the underlined words.

   <u>Seagulls</u> flew over the ocean.   _____

   <u>Jonathon</u> had to get up early.   _____

8. Write the two words that make up each contraction.

   couldn't ➡ _____ + _____

   don't ➡ _____ + _____

Lesson #21

1. Choose the correct homophone.

   I want to (by / buy) a hotdog at the game.

   I asked to sit (by / buy) myself.

2. Read each sentence. Look for the exact words someone says. Put quotation marks before and after what they say.

   Holly said, I can't wait for the first snowfall!

   Ben asked, Would you help me with my homework?

3. Circle the words with a short vowel sound.

   hopped   take

   fly   skip   hot

4. Write the mark for "make capital." _____

5. Underline the predicate of the sentence.

   Amanda brought a treat to school for her birthday.

6. Write the verb from the sentence in item #5.

   _____

7. Which word has a spelling mistake? Write it correctly.

   wished   cryed   laughed

   _____

8. Write this sentence correctly.

   <u>m</u>r. Thomas is∧ baseball coach⊙
                  our

   _____

   _____

Lesson #22

1. Choose the correct verb.

   Jen (see / saw) a fox in the woods.

   She has (saw / seen) deer in the woods, too.

2. Look for the exact words someone says. Put quotation marks before and after what they say.

   Rachael said, I am thirsty.

   Ricardo asked, Can you fix my bicycle?

3. Which word means the opposite of the word *late*?

   end   early   next

4. Write the mark for "make lower case."

   _____

Summer Solutions© Grammar & Writing   Level 2

5 – 6. Read the sentences below. Find four mistakes. Use the special marks to show how to fix the sentences.

I like going to school   my Favorite class is math.

My teacher really nice. I have a lot of friends.

7. Write the sentence that has no mistake in items 5 – 6.

_____

_____

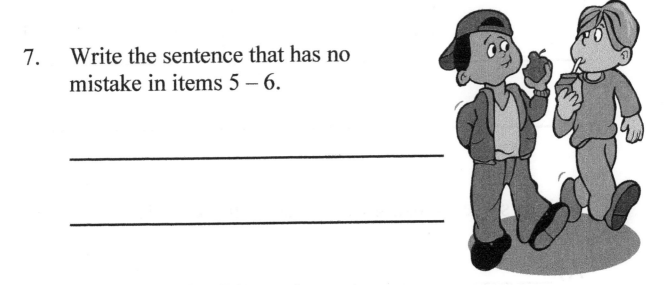

8. Circle the correct adjective.

Your house is (bigger / biggest) than mine.

My neighbor has the (prettier / prettiest) flowers in her yard.

Lesson #23

1. Draw a picture of a person, a place, and a thing. Write the noun that names the picture on the line.

A) person	B) place	C) thing

   _____   _____   _____

2. Write a sentence using each noun from item #1.

   A) _____

   B) _____

   C) _____

3. Fill in the correct end mark.

   My brother wants a snake__

   Will it live in a cage__   I hate snakes__

4. Use an *apostrophe* + -*s* (*'s*) to show ownership.

   The motorcycle belongs to Uncle Mike. It is Uncle Mike__ motorcycle.

5. Circle the adjective that describes each underlined word.

   Mr. Kwan took a huge <u>suitcase</u> on the plane.

   Pablo left his wet <u>towel</u> on the bed.

6 – 8. Write three sentences comparing these two dogs. Use comparing words ending in –*er*.

 Max  Muffin

_____

_____

_____

_____

Lesson #24

1. Choose the correct homophone.

   Jay knew the (right / write) answer.

   Mr. Wilson had to (right / write) a letter to the bank.

2. Underline the verb in the action part of the sentence.

   The astronauts climbed into the spacecraft.

3. What is the subject in the above sentence?

   _____

4. Add -s or -es to make these nouns name more than one.

   ash__   cage__   bush__   pond__

5 – 6. **When you use quotation marks around what someone says**
   a) Always put a **comma after** words like *said* and *asked*.
   b) Begin the **first word inside** the quotation marks with a **capital letter**.
   c) Put the **end mark inside the quotation marks**.

   Use the rules above to fix these sentences.

   A) Monica said   "Today is my birthday."

   B) Jake asked,   "when are we going to eat?"

   C) My dad said, "I have to fly to New York".

7. Add the suffix *-less* to the word *home* to make a word that means "without a home."

   home + -less ➡ _____

8. Circle the correct verb.

   She (is / are) a great swimmer.

   We (am / are) best friends.

Lesson #25

1. Read each sentence. Look for the exact words someone says. Always put a comma after words like *said* and *asked*. Put quotation marks before and after what they say.

   Use the rules above to fix these sentences.

   The woman asked   Have you seen my cat?

   Willie said   My shoes are full of mud.

2. Choose the correct verb.

   Marcie (help / helped) her dad cut the grass.

   She (has / have) helped him shovel snow, too.

3. Write the two words that make up the compound word below.

   breakfast ➡ _____ + _____

4. Write the mark that means "add a period."

   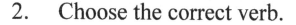

5. Write a pronoun that can replace the underlined words.

   <u>The game</u> started early. _____

   <u>The kitten and puppy</u> played on the rug. _____

6. Underline the words that should begin with a capital letter.

   florida   november

   church   cleveland

7. **When you write the title of a book, make the first letter of every important word in the title a capital letter. Draw a line under the title.**

   Example: <u>The Lion, the Witch, and the Wardrobe</u>

   Underline each title. Use the mark for "make capital" to show which words should be capitalized in these titles.

   ira sleeps over   charlotte's web

8. Write the mark for "take something out."

   _____

Lesson #26

1. Choose the correct homophone.

   We went on (our / hour) family vacation.

   Our flight took us only one (our / hour).

2. Underline the book titles below.

   Curious George   The Giving Tree

3. Underline the predicate, or action part of the sentence.

   Dolphins live in the ocean.

4. Put in a comma after the word *said* or *asked* and put quotation marks around what the person said.

   My dad asked   Is anyone going to cut the grass?

Summer Solutions® Grammar & Writing Level 2

5. Add the prefix *re–* to the word *try* to make a word that means "to try again."

re- + try ➡ _____

6 – 7. Put the nouns in the Word Box into the correct column.

| boat | notebook | church | nurse | baby |
| bank | magazine | forest | girl | carrot |

People	Places	Things

8. Underline the subject.

The elephant is from Africa.

53

Lesson #27

1. Replace the underlined words with a contraction.

   Some people <u>do not</u> have computers. _____

   Alvin <u>is not</u> afraid of spiders. _____

2. Underline the book titles.

   Tales of a Fourth Grade Nothing

   Little House in the Big Woods

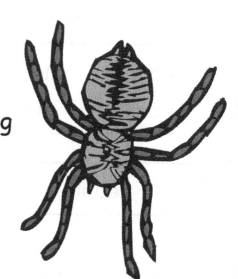

3. Choose the correct verb.

   I (kick / kicks) the ball and run to the base.

   Chris (catch / catches) the ball and throws me out.

4. Circle the adjective that describes the underlined word.

   My <u>clothes</u> smell fresh.

   The kitten had wet <u>paws</u>.

5. Use the mark for "make capital" and "take something out" to fix this sentence.

   Mrs. mason drove me to the the dentist.

6. Underline the predicate of the sentence. Circle the verb.

   I ate a soft pretzel for snack today.

7. Underline the sentence.

   Fell down.

   I had to do the dishes.

   Her mother.

8. Write your own sentence about a job you do at home.

   _____

   _____

   _____

Lesson #28

1. Fill in a word to describe each noun below. The word can describe how something looks, feels, smells, or tastes.

   _____ monkey   _____ sugar

2. Choose the correct homophone.

   (To / Two) wasps flew by my head.

   I didn't want (to / two) get stung.

3. Underline the proper nouns.

   Marissa went to Georgia with Aunt Donna.

4. For these nouns that name more than one, add an *apostrophe* after the *-s* (*s'*) to show ownership.

   bees_ honey

   horses_ hay

5. Put quotation marks around what each person is saying. Make sure to put a comma after the word *said* or *asked*.

   Mom asked   Do you want to have your friend sleep over?

   Rose said   I will call Megan right now.

6. Write the two words that make up this compound word.

   fruitcake ➡ _____ + _____

7. Underline two *antonyms* or words that mean the opposite.

   short   find   long   begin

8. Your birthday is coming up. Fill in some things you might ask for as gifts.

Lesson #29

1. Which part of the sentence is underlined?

   <u>The clown</u> gave us each a balloon.

   predicate   subject

2. Underline the book titles in this sentence.

   Two of my favorite books are Nate the Great and Mr. Popper's Penguins.

3. Write a pronoun to replace each underlined word.

   <u>Tina</u> plays the guitar. _____

   <u>Mitch</u> plays the drums. _____

4. Which word is a *synonym* for (means almost the same as) the word *jump*?

   trip   fall   leap

5. Put quotation marks around what each person says.

My teacher asked, What is the sum of seven and six?

6. Underline the nouns that name people.

My sister is a doctor.

7. Write 4 adjectives to describe yourself.

   Examples: funny, kind, smart, strong

   _____   _____

   _____   _____

8. Choose the correct verb.

Mr. Jax (was / were) my dad's boss.

Lesson #30

1. Rewrite the underlined words as contractions. (Use the *Help Pages* if you need to.)

   I <u>cannot</u> jump rope. _____

   I <u>do not</u> want to tell the teacher. _____

2. Circle the adjective that describes the underlined word.

   Toucans have colorful <u>beaks</u>.

   Tina saw eight <u>ants</u> on the floor.

3. Which word has a spelling mistake? Write the correct spelling on the line.

   sound   anything   lauf

   _____

4. Write the mark for "add a period." _____

5. Underline the book title.

   Lisa read Huckleberry Finn over the summer.

6. Fill in the correct end mark.

   That's great___

   Give the dog a bath___

   Did you eat all of your lunch___

7 – 8. Read the sentences. Find four mistakes and show how to fix the mistakes using the special marks.

   toucans live in the rain forest   They nest and

   sleep inside tree Trunks. Toucans eat berries,

   seeds, small insects, birds.

Summer Solutions® Grammar & Writing — Level 2

level 2

English Grammar
& Writing Mechanics

Help Pages

Help Pages

Kinds of Sentences:		
Statement	tells something	.
Question	asks something	?
Command	tells someone to do something	.
Exclamation	shows emotion	!

Editing Marks:	
Capital letter	≡
End Punctuation	⊙ ! ?
Add Something	∧
Change to lower case	/
Take something out	⌒
Indent	¶

Helping Verbs:
have
has

Steps in the Writing Process:		
1.	Prewriting	getting ideas for writing
2.	Drafting	putting your ideas into writing
3.	Revising	adding or taking out to make your writing better
4.	Editing	using editing marks to correct mistakes
5.	Publishing	sharing your writing with others

Help Pages

Rules for Spelling:
1. Words ending in *s, x, z, ch,* or *sh,* add *-es* to make the plural.
2. To make compound words, usually join two words without changing the spelling of either word.
3. When adding a suffix to a word, the spelling of the word sometimes changes; the suffix does not usually change.
4. When a word ends in a consonant plus *y,* change the *y* to *i* and add *-es.*
5. If a word ends in *-e* and you want to add a suffix that begins with a vowel, drop the *-e* before adding the suffix.

Subject Pronouns:	
Singular	I, you, he, she, it
Plural	we, you, they

Prefixes:
un- means "not"
re- means "again"
pre- means "before"

Contractions:	
cannot / can not	can't
do not	don't
does not	doesn't
is not	isn't

Suffixes:
-er means "someone who does something"
-ful means "full of"
-less means "without"

Help Pages

Vocabulary:	
Sentence	a group of words that tells a complete thought
Naming / Subject	tells who or what the sentence is about
Action/Predicate	tells what the subject does or is
Synonym	a word that means the same or almost the same as another word
Antonym	a word that means the opposite of another word
Homophone	words that sound alike but have different spellings and meanings

Parts of Speech:	
Noun	a word that names a person, place, or thing
Verb	a word that shows action or a state of being; a verb is the main word in the action part of the sentence
Pronoun	a word that takes the place of a noun
Adjective	a word that describes a noun

Rules for Using Capital Letters:	
The beginning of every sentence	Names of special people, places, or things
Every time you use "I"	Important words in a book title
Months of the year	Titles of people
Holidays	Days of the week

Help Pages

Verb Tenses:	
Present Time Verbs	Most present time verbs end in –s when the subject is singular. (Kim <u>bakes</u> cookies every day.)
Past Time Verbs	Verbs that tell an action that has already happened usually add –ed to show past time. (Kim <u>baked</u> a pie yesterday.)

Irregular Verbs:		
Present	**Past**	**With *has* or *have***
come	came	*has or have* come
do	did	*has or have* done
give	gave	*has or have* given
go	went	*has or have* gone
run	ran	*has or have* run
see	saw	*has or have* seen

Rules for Showing Ownership:	
Single noun	Add an apostrophe + -s
Noun that names more than one	Add an apostrophe after the -s

Rules for Using Quotation Marks:
- Use quotation marks (" ") around what someone says.
- Always put a comma after words like <u>said</u> and <u>asked</u>.
- Begin a sentence inside quotation marks with a capital letter.
- Put the end mark inside the quotation marks.

Summer Solutions© Grammar & Writing Level 2

level 2

English Grammar
& Writing Mechanics

Answers to Lessons

	Lesson #1		Lesson #2		Lesson #3
1	<u>A baby frog</u>	1	<u>plays the drums.</u>	1	<u>talks to us.</u>
2	<u>heavy</u> <u>light</u>	2	uneasy	2	<u>The children</u>
3	crashed smelled	3	"Make your bed before we go." "Can I play with you?"	3	picture
4	driving giving	4	sea + shore	4	=
5	capital	5	smaller smallest	5	eight ate
6	We are getting a swimming pool in June.	6	...hammer? ...camera. ...picture!	6	does + not do + not
7	<u>gave</u> <u>done</u>	7	chubby, cute, furry, tall, short,... Answers will vary.	7	The nurse asked, "How are you feeling?"
8	(huge)	8	Answers will vary.	8	spotless

	Lesson #4		Lesson #5		Lesson #6
1	ran up the tree.	1	Monica asked, "How old is your dog?" I answered, "He's five years old."	1	ponies pennies
2	The path was narrow.	2	loves to play video games	2	rode
3	Answers will vary.	3	is are	3	doesn't can't
4	(yellow) jacket (spotted) whale	4	berry	4	pals
5	Some animals	5	My sister and I	5	(throws) (drives)
6	(easy) (simple)	6	I like to eat fries with ^my hamburger⊙	6	My t~~he~~ dog always barks at strangers ⊙
7	Answers will vary.	7	(loud) voice (silver) truck	7	My dog always barks at strangers.
8	Answers will vary.	8	beaches couches	8	am was

Lesson #7		Lesson #8		Lesson #9	
1	hairless	1	Erin's	1	dancer
2	puppies bunnies	2	<u>I'll also bring the sweeper</u>.	2	...here? ...birds.
3	<u>The baby</u>	3	<u>We</u> <u>She</u>	3	hobbies
4	news + paper	4	doesn't don't	4	<u>Susie and I jumped rope</u>.
5	(did) (done)	5	gave (had) given	5	mail + box
6	coat toad	6	playful	6	¶ Jared found a dollar on the ground...
7	<u>bird</u> <u>nest</u>	7	<u>(tossed) the football to me</u>.	7	He
8	It	8	¶	8	Darla bought a book about birds⊙ <u>s</u>he read ten pages as soon as she∧ home. got

	Lesson #10		Lesson #11		Lesson #12
1	Answers will vary.	1	cake – sweet apple – juicy	1	pizza – hot or spicy nose – wet or hot
2	Answers will vary.	2	pickle – sour chili sauce – hot (Answers may vary.)	2	seashells beach
3	my memorial day	3	girls' birds'	3	sea + shells
4	mother	4	pencils dishes	4	true
5	My mom	5	sprayed	5	am were
6	light	6	swing	6	can't isn't
7	using smiling	7	Answers will vary.	7	capital
8	Leo Jackson Ohio	8	Answers will vary.	8	⊙

	Lesson #13		Lesson #14		Lesson #15
1	It	1	has	1	faster fastest
2	Jake has a soccer game on Sunday.	2	Answers will vary.	2	april monday christmas
3	(quick)	3	goat tired	3	saving waving
4	cooked turkey for dinner.	4	...game. or game! ...go?	4	Dexter's
5	cooked	5	A) Yes B) No C) No D) Yes	5	Emily → She The kite → It
6	Answers will vary.	6	the monkey swung from ∧ tree. the (or a)	6	daisies bodies
7	resay	7	The monkey swung from the tree.	7	(spicy) - tacos table - (sticky)
8	Bring your money tomorrow.	8	Tyrone Dr. Kendall	8	flower - (sweet) (sour) - candy

Summer Solutions© Grammar & Writing — Level 2

Lesson #16		Lesson #17		Lesson #18	
1	bigger biggest	1	(awake)	1	helpful
2	¶	2	action part	2	blew won
3	have has	3	The turtle moved slowly across ∧ yard. (the)	3	∧
4	watched	4	The turtle moved slowly across the yard.	4	¶ We heard Sal blow the whistle ⊙
5	Jerry and I play basketball.	5	Mr. Williams is my football coach.	5	Answers will vary.
6	matches friends	6	softer softest	6	hot or cold
7	preheat	7	boys softball bats gloves field	7	hot, cold or green green or cold
8	busy	8	brought	8	is am

	Lesson #19		Lesson #20		Lesson #21
1	clothes flour	1	(angry)	1	buy by
2	<u>played</u> <u>wag</u>	2	has have	2	"I can't wait for the first snowfall!" "Would you help me with my homework?"
3	isn't	3	(clean) <u>sheets</u> (silky) <u>hair</u>	3	(hopped) (skip) (hot)
4	joking baking	4	rail + road	4	=
5 - 8	Answers will vary.	5	hear	5	<u>brought a treat to school for her birthday</u>.
		6	clueless	6	brought
		7	They He	7	cried
		8	could + not do + not	8	Mr. Thomas is our baseball coach.

Lesson #22		Lesson #23		Lesson #24	
1	saw seen	1	Answers will vary.	1	right write
2	"I am thirsty." "Can you fix my bicycle?"	2	Answers will vary.	2	climbed
3	early	3	...snake. ...cage? ...snakes!	3	The astronauts
4	/	4	Uncle Mike's	4	ashes cages bushes ponds
5-6	I like going to school⊙ <u>my</u>/Favorite class is math. My teacher ∧ really nice. is	5	(huge) suitcase (wet) towel	5-6	A) Monica said, ... B) Jake asked, "When ... C) "I have to fly to New York."
7	I have a lot of friends.	6-8	Answers will vary.	7	homeless
8	bigger prettiest			8	(is) (are)

	Lesson #25		Lesson #26		Lesson #27
1	The woman asked, "Have you seen my cat?" Willie said, "My shoes are full of mud."	1	our hour	1	don't isn't
2	helped has	2	<u>Curious George</u> <u>The Giving Tree</u>	2	<u>Tales of a Fourth Grade Nothing</u> <u>Little House in the Big Woods</u>
3	break + fast	3	<u>live in the ocean.</u>	3	kick catches
4	⊙	4	My dad asked, "Is anyone going to cut the grass?"	4	<u>clothes</u> (fresh) (wet) paws
5	It They	5	retry	5	Mrs. mason drove me to the the dentist.
6	<u>florida</u> <u>november</u> <u>cleveland</u>	6	People: nurse, baby, girl Places: church, bank, forest Things: notebook, boat, carrot, magazine	6	(ate) <u>a soft pretzel for snack today.</u>
7	<u>ira sleeps over</u> <u>charlotte's web</u>	7		7	<u>I had to do the dishes.</u>
8	ʠ	8	<u>The elephant</u>	8	Answers will vary.

Summer Solutions© Grammar & Writing — Level 2

	Lesson #28		Lesson #29		Lesson #30
1	Answers will vary.	1	subject	1	can't don't
2	Two to	2	<u>Nate the Great</u> <u>Mr. Popper's</u> <u>Penguins</u>	2	(colorful) (eight)
3	<u>Marissa</u> <u>Georgia</u> <u>Aunt Donna</u>	3	She He	3	laugh
4	bees' horses'	4	leap	4	⊙
5	Mom asked, "Do you want to have your friend sleep over?" Rose said, "I will call Megan right now."	5	My teacher asked, "What is the sum of seven and six?"	5	<u>Huckleberry Finn</u>
6	fruit + cake	6	<u>sister</u> <u>doctor</u>	6	...great! ...bath. ...lunch?
7	<u>short</u> <u>long</u>	7	Answers will vary.	7 – 8	toucans forest⊙ Trunks insects, ∧ birds. and
8	Answers will vary.	8	was		